Stirring

MOCK

Published 2008 by
Prakash Books India Pvt. Ltd.
1, Ansari Road, Daryaganj
New Delhi 110 002, India.
E-mail: sales@prakashbooks.com
Website: www.prakashbooks.com
Tel: 91-11-23247062-65

© 2008 Prakash Books India Pvt. Ltd.

STAR © Rasoi is a property of STAR India Pvt. Ltd.

All rights reserved. No part of this publication may be reproduced, stored in a retrieval system or transmitted in any form or by any means, electronic, mechanical, photocopying, recording or otherwise, without the prior permission of the copyright holder.

ISBN: 978-81-7234-271-5

Printed & bound in India at: Presstech Litho Pvt. Ltd.

Stirring Tales!

MOCKTAILS

STAR Rasoi

Inspired by STAR TV Shows

Contents

1. *Designated Appletini* 8
2. *Cherry Ale* 11
3. *Virgin Miami Vice* 12
4. *Berry Sweetheart* 13
5. *Orange Julius* 14
6. *Beach Blanket Bingo* 15
7. *Green Grape Glacier* 16
8. *Strawberry Julius* 17
9. *Cran-Dandy Cooler* 18
10. *Spiced Tomato Juice* 21
11. *Coco Colada* 22
12. *Virgin Sling* 23
13. *Apple Julep* 24
14. *Mint Julep* 25
15. *Mock Champagne* 26
16. *Italian Cream Soda* 27
17. *Apricot Mocktail* 28
18. *Mock Sangria* 31
19. *Colossal Pina Colada* 32
20. *Peach Daiquiri* 33
21. *Lady Rose* 34
22. *Virgin Mary* 37
23. *Backyard Berry Sun Tea* 38
24. *Cinderella* 39
25. *Spring Fever* 40
26. *Sundowner* 41
27. *Lemon Punch* 42
28. *Vienna Soother* 45
29. *Baby Bellini* 46
30. *Roogeltea* 47
31. *The Tropical Spritzer* 48
32. *Virgin Mango Bellini* 51
33. *The English Garden Sipper* 52
34. *The Berry Patch* 53
35. *Hot Fudge Sundae* 54
36. *Virgin Strawberry Daiquiri* 55
37. *Quiet Passion* 56
38. *Bikini Breezer* 57
39. *Fruity Punch* 58
40. *Unfuzzy Navel* 59
41. *Tequila Meadow* 60

Introduction

It's party time once again. And you've got it all set up for your guests. The food is superb; the liquor is of the finest quality. The snacks are out of this world.

Wait a minute. What are you going to serve people who don't drink alcohol? Flavoured soda again? Aerated water? Oh, come on. Surely they deserve better than that.

How about whipping up an interesting mocktail instead? A lovely blend of juices and other ingredients without a touch of alcohol. Sounds good doesn't it?

Sip on an exquisite 'mocktail' – a mixture of fruit juices, flavors and garnishes. A sort of rum punch without the rum, but certainly with a lot of punch and served in stylish cocktail glasses.

Mocktails are festive, non-alcoholic party drinks. Mocktails are often offered for designated drivers, pregnant women, or any party guests who choose not to drink alcohol. Although many drink recipes can be prepared without alcohol, some are especially popular. Mocktails come in many varieties: frozen, hot, fizzy, non-fizzy, and cream-based recipes.

The term Mocktail was created by John Doxat, author of The Complete Drinkers Companion, which was published in 1985 by Grafton Books.

A Shirley Temple or sometimes called virgin sling is one of the classic mocktails, often served to children. Named for the child actor, it contains lemon-lime soda, ginger ale, and a dash of grenadine, with a maraschino cherry for garnish. The Roy Rogers is another of the traditional mocktails, this one named for a straight-laced singing cowboy; it is made with cola splashed with a bit of grenadine and is also garnished with a maraschino cherry.

Any flavor of Daiquiri can be made into a mocktail. For a raspberry non-alcoholic version, blend ice, raspberry puree, and lime juice; pour into a glass with sugar on the rim and garnish with fresh raspberries. To create a Seabreeze mocktail, mix cranberry juice, grapefruit juice, and a little lime juice. Using a chilled highball glass, pour the mixed juices over ice.

A Nada Colada contains all the ingredients of a regular Pina Colada except the alcohol. Blend pineapple juice, cream of coconut, rum extract, and crushed ice in a blender until smooth. Serve garnished with a pineapple slice. The Cajun Clamato is a mock bloody-Mary type drink made with Clamato juice, a dash each of Worcestershire sauce and Tabasco, salt and pepper, horseradish, and a celery stalk for garnish.

Mocktails are popular alternatives to alcoholic drinks and allow everyone to enjoy the spirit of a celebratory occasion in a responsible manner. Most mocktails are blends of fresh fruit juices and syrups, and some contain cream, herbs, or spices. Since mocktails contain no alcohol, people of all ages can enjoy them.

Designated Appletini

Ingredients:

Freshly pressed apple juice (green or gold apples)	: 60 ml
Sugar syrup	: 15 ml
Lemon juice	: 8 ml

For sugar syrup:

Sugar	: 2 parts
Water	: 1 part

Procedure:
1) Add apple juice, sugar syrup and lemon juice to a cocktail shaker filled with ice.
2) Shake well.
3) Strain into a chilled cocktail glass.

For sugar syrup:
1) Bring the water to a boil.
2) Dissolve the sugar into the boiling water.
3) Once the sugar is dissolved completely, remove the pan from the heat.
4) Allow to cool completely and bottle.

Cherry Ale

Ingredients:

Cherry Juice	: 60 ml	Dash of Grenadine
Lime Cordial	: 15 ml	Ginger Ale

Procedure:

1) Fill a tall glass with ice.
2) Add the cherry juice, and lime cordial, add a dash of grenadine and top with ginger ale.
3) If desired garnish with a maraschino cherry.

Virgin Miami Vice

Ingredients:

Pineapple juice	: 30 ml	Lime juice	: 45 ml
Coconut cream	: 30 ml	Sugar syrup	: 8 ml
Light cream	: 15 ml	Ice, crushed	: 1 cup
Strawberry puree	: 45 ml	Strawberry for garnish	

Procedure:
1) Place the pineapple juice, coconut cream, cream and a half a cup of ice into a blender.
2) Blend the mixture until smooth.
3) Pour the mixture into a highball glass.
4) Place the strawberry puree, lime juice, sugar syrup and the remaining half cup of ice into a blender.
5) Blend the mixture until smooth.
6) Slowly pour the strawberry-lime mixture over the back of a barspoon on top of the pineapple-coconut mixture. Your mocktail is ready.

To serve: *Garnish with a strawberry.*

Berry Sweetheart

Ingredients:

Red cranberry juice	: 90 ml	Honey	: 30 ml
Apple juice	: 90 ml	Cherry for garnish	

Procedure:
1) Fill a highball glass with ice cubes.
2) Add the juices and honey to a mixing glass.
3) Stir the ingredients with a barspoon.
4) Pour the contents of the mixing glass into the highball glass.

To serve: Garnish with a cherry.

Orange Julius

The Orange Julius is one of the classic blended mocktails that you probably remember from childhood. It's a delicious frozen drink that is sure to chill you out on the hottest days of the year.

Ingredients:

Fresh or frozen orange juice : 1 cup	Vanilla extract : 1 tsp
or Orange juice concentrate : 120 ml	Sugar : 2 tbsp
Milk : 60 ml	Vanilla ice cream : 1 scoop

Procedure:

1) Place all ingredients in a blender with ½ cup of ice.
2) Blend until smooth.
3) Pour into a chilled hurricane glass.
4) If the mix is too thick, add more juice or water.

Beach Blanket Bingo

Ingredients:

Grapefruit juice	: 90 ml	Soda water	
Cranberry juice	: 90 ml	Lime wedge for garnish	

Procedure:

1) Pour the juices into a collins glass filled with ice.
2) Pour the soda water on top.
3) Garnish with a lime wedge.

Green Grape Glacier

Yummy!! If you are a fan of green grapes this is the mocktail for you. Wonderful for a morning drink or an afternoon at the beach, a Green Grape Glacier is a luxurious treat and the frozen grapes for the garnish are an extra bonus.

Ingredients:

Seedless green grapes	: 12	
White grape juice	: 120 ml	
Cold sparkling water	: 120 ml	

Procedure:

1) Freeze the grapes until hard.
2) Combine 10 frozen grapes and grape juice in a blender and mix for about 20 seconds or until smooth and thick.
3) Pour the grape mix into glass.
4) Add the sparkling water.
5) Stir gently.
6) Garnish with the remaining 2 frozen grapes.

Strawberry Julius

This is a strawberry flavored variation of the classic Orange Julius. It is a delicious blended cocktails that is great in summer.

Ingredients:

Fresh or frozen strawberry juice	: 1 cup	Sugar	: 2 tbsp
Milk	: 60 ml	Vanilla ice cream	: 1 scoop
Vanilla extract	: 1 tsp	Strawberry for garnish	

Procedure:

1) Place all ingredients in a blender with ½ cup of ice.
2) Blend until smooth.
3) Pour into a chilled hurricane glass.
4) If the mix is too thick, add more juice or water.

Cran-Dandy Cooler

"A carbonated cranberry and pineapple refreshing cooler."

Ingredients:

cranberry juice	: 2 cups	lemon juice	: 2 tbsp
pineapple juice	: 1 cup	ginger ale	: 360 ml
orange juice	: 1 cup	orange, sliced in rounds	: 1

Procedure:

1) In a gallon pitcher combine cranberry juice, pineapple juice, orange juice and lemon juice.
2) Just before serving, slowly add ginger ale; stir to blend.
3) Serve over ice in cups or glasses.
4) If desired garnish with orange slices.

Spiced Tomato Juice

Ingredients:

Tomato juice	: 2 bottles (32 ounce each)	Pepper	: 1 tsp
Lemon juice	: ½ cup	Salt	: 1 tsp
Lime juice	: ¼ cup	Hot pepper sauce	: ⅛ tsp
Worcestershire sauce	: 2 tbsp	Celery ribs with leaves	: 8 med.

Procedure:

1) In a large pitcher, combine the first seven ingredients; stir well.
2) Pour into glasses and garnish with celery if desired.
3) Serve immediately.

Coco Colada

A Coco Colada is a great non-alcoholic version of the Frozen Piña Colada.

Ingredients:

Pineapple juice	: 120 ml	Ice	: 1 cup
Coconut cream	: 20 ml	Orange slice for garnish	
or Piña colada mix	: 180 ml		

Procedure:

1) In a blender, add 1 cup ice, pineapple juice and cream of coconut (or piña colada mix).
2) Blend until slushy.
3) Pour into an chilled hurricane glass.

Virgin Sling
(Also called Shirley Temple)

Ingredients:

Lemon Juice	: 90 ml	Grenadine	: a dash
Orange Juice	: 60 ml	Ginger Ale	: 100 ml or as required

Procedure:
1) Shake the Lemon Juice and Orange Juice with ice in a cocktail shaker,
2) Pour into a sling glass.
3) Add a dash of Grenadine and top up the glass with Ginger Ale.

Apple Julep

Ingredients:

Apple juice	: 1 litre	Lemon juice	: ¼ cup
Orange juice	: 1 cup	Fresh mint leaves	: 1 sprig
Pineapple juice	: 1 cup		

Procedure:
1) In a large pitcher, stir together the apple juice, orange juice, pineapple juice and lemon juice.
2) Before serving pour into glasses full of ice.
3) Garnish each serving with a mint leaf.

Mint Julep

Ingredients:

Water	: ¼ cup	Crushed ice	: 2 cups
Sugar	: ¼ cup	Prepared lemonade	: ½ cup
Chopped fresh mint leaves	: 1 tbsp		

Procedure:

1) In a small saucepan, combine the water, sugar and chopped mint leaves. Stir and bring to a boil.
2) Cook until sugar has dissolved, then remove from heat and set aside to cool.
3) After about an hour, strain out mint leaves.
4) Fill 2 cups or glasses with crushed ice. Pour ½ cup lemonade into each glass and top with a splash of the mint sugar syrup.

Mock Champagne

Ingredients:

Sugar	: ⅔ cup	Orange juice	: ½ cup
Water	: ⅔ cup	Grenadine syrup	: 3 tbsp
Grapefruit juice	: 1 cup	Ginger ale (chilled)	: 840 ml

Procedure:
1) Combine sugar and water in saucepan over low heat.
2) Stir until sugar is dissolved.
3) Bring to boil and boil for 10 minutes.
4) Then set it cool.
5) Now add sugar syrup and juices together and chill throughly.
6) Top with grenadine and ginger ale just before serving.
7) Serve chilled.

Italian Cream Soda

"A watermelon and passion fruit flavored Italian cream soda."

Ingredients:

Carbonated water	: 240 ml	Watermelon flavored syrup	: 25 ml
Passion fruit flavored syrup	: 25 ml	Light cream	: 30 ml

Procedure:
1) Take a tall glass, fill it half with ice.
2) Fill another ⅔ with carbonated water.
3) Pour the watermelon and passion fruit syrups and then gently pour the light cream on top.
4) Stir when ready to drink.

Note:
- You can use any fruit syrups to make your Italian cream soda.

Apricot Mocktail

Ingredients:

Apricot juice	: 60 ml	Grenadine	: 1 tsp
Orange juice	: 60 ml	Lime juice.	: 8 ml

Procedure:
1) Put all the ingredients in a cocktail shaker filled with ice.
2) Shake and strain into a martini glass.

Mock Sangria

Ingredients:

Purple, red, or white grape juice (chilled)	: 2 bottles 720 ml each
Club soda (chilled)	: 1 litre
Pineapple (cut bite-size)	: ½ small
Orange (sliced)	: 1 large
Ice cubes	: 1 tray

Procedure:
1) In pitcher, combine juice and soda.
2) Add fruit on top along with ice cubes.

Note:
- You can also use apples (cut bite size) instead of pineapple.

Colossal Pina Colada

Ingredients:

Skim milk	: 2 cups	Coconut extract	: 1 tbsp
Unsweetened pineapple juice	: 2 cups	Sugar	: 2 tbsp
Vanilla extract	: 1 tbsp	Ice cubes	
		Mint sprigs for garnish	

Procedure:
1) Combine all ingredients, except ice cubes & mint, in a blender and blend on high speed until frothy.
2) Pour into 6 tall glasses filled with ice cubes.
3) Garnish with mint sprigs, if desired.

Procedure for thicker variation:
1) Omit ice cubes and freeze the pineapple juice in ice-cube trays.
2) Then blend these cubes with the other ingredients and garnish with mint.

Peach Daiquiri

Ingredients:

Peaches (drain the juice to make)	: 420 ml	Milk	: ⅛ cup
Lemon juice	: 1 tbsp	Peach juice	: ½ cup
Ice cubes	: 6	Rum flavoring	: ½ tsp

Procedure:
1) Put peaches, lemon juice, ice cubes, milk, peach juice and rum flavoring into a blender.
2) Blend until ice is gone.
3) Serve immediately.

Note:
- Since fresh peaches are being used, you can add sugar, 1 tbsp or to taste.

Lady Rose

Ingredients:

Rose water	: 2 tbsp	Ice cubes	: 6
Lemon juice	: 2 tbsp	Water	: ½ cup
Grenadine	: 1 tbsp	Red/pink food colour	: a dash
Sugar, granulated	: 1 tbsp		

Procedure:
1) Mix water/rose water, lemon juice, grenadine, sugar, food colour and ice cubes into blender.
2) Blend until ice is gone.
3) Serve immediately.

Virgin Mary

Ingredients:

Tomato juice	: 180ml	Lime juice	: a dash
Worsteschire	: a dash	Salt to taste	
Tabasco	: a dash	Pepper to taste	

Procedure:

1) Mix all the ingredients with ice and blend in a blender.
2) If desired garnish with a Celery stalk & Lime wedge.

Backyard Berry Sun Tea

(Preparation for a small gathering or a party)

Ingredients:

Cold water	: 3 litres	Granulated sugar to taste	
Raspberry tea	: 8 bags	limes, sliced	: 2
Sparkling raspberry juice	: 1 litre	Fresh raspberries	: 1 small carton

Procedure:
1) Pour water in a jug.
2) Add tea bags.
3) Place in direct sunlight for 8 hours.
4) Remove tea bags and add raspberry juice and sugar.
5) Pour over ice and garnish with a lime wheel and raspberries if desired.

Cinderella

Ingredients:

Pineapple juice	: 60 ml	Grenadine	: a dash
Orange juice	: 60 ml	Ice cubes	: a few
Lemon juice	: 60 ml	Orange & pineapple slices	
Club Soda	: 120 ml	for garnishing	

Procedure:

1) Put some ice cubes in a shaker and pour all the juices into it.
2) Shake it well.
3) Strain into a chilled cocktail glass.
4) Add club soda and then grenadine.
5) Garnish with orange and pineapple slices.
6) Serve it chilled.

Spring Fever

Ingredients:

Lemon Juice	: 25 ml	Orange juice	: 60 ml
Mango juice or syrup	: 25 ml	Ice cubes	: a few
Pineapple juice	: 45 ml		

Procedure:
1) Put some ice cubes in a shaker.
2) Now add all the ingredients into the shaker.
3) Shake it well.
4) Strain into a glass half filled with crushed ice.
5) Serve it chilled.

Sundowner

Ingredients:

White Grape juice	: 60 ml	Fresh mint for garnishing
Cold sparkling water	: 40 ml	
Ice cubes	: a few	

Procedure:

1) Pour the ingredients into a wine glass with ice.
2) Stir and garnish it with mint.
3) Serve it chilled.

Lemon Punch

Ingredients:

Honey	: 20 ml	Salt to taste
Sweet Lime juice	: 100 ml	Crushed ice
Orange Juice	: 60 ml	A slice of lime for garnishing
Lime Juice	: ½ tsp	

Procedure:
1) Put honey in a ribbed glass.
2) Add the sweet lime juice.
3) Add orange juice, lime juice and salt.
4) Stir once.
5) Top with crushed ice.
6) Garnish with a slice of sweet lime.

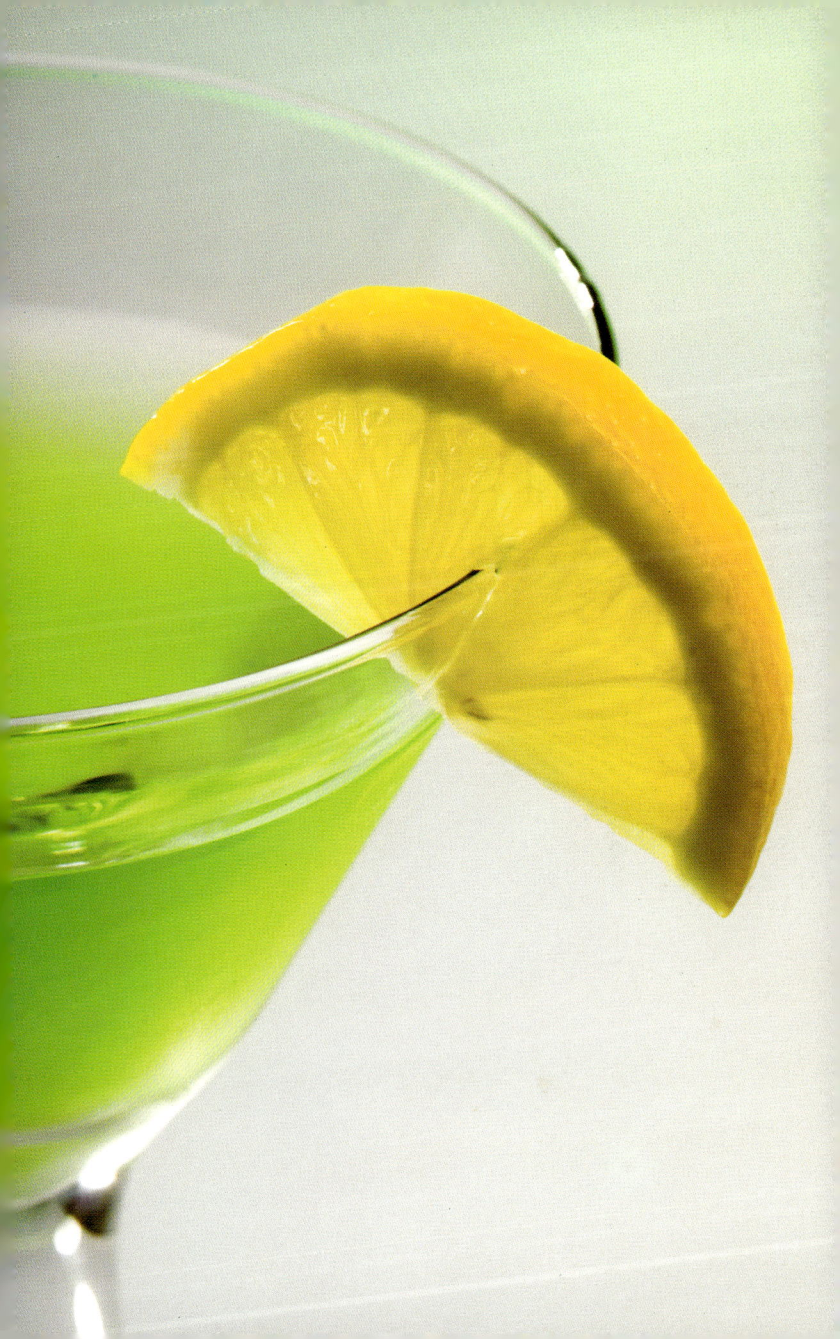

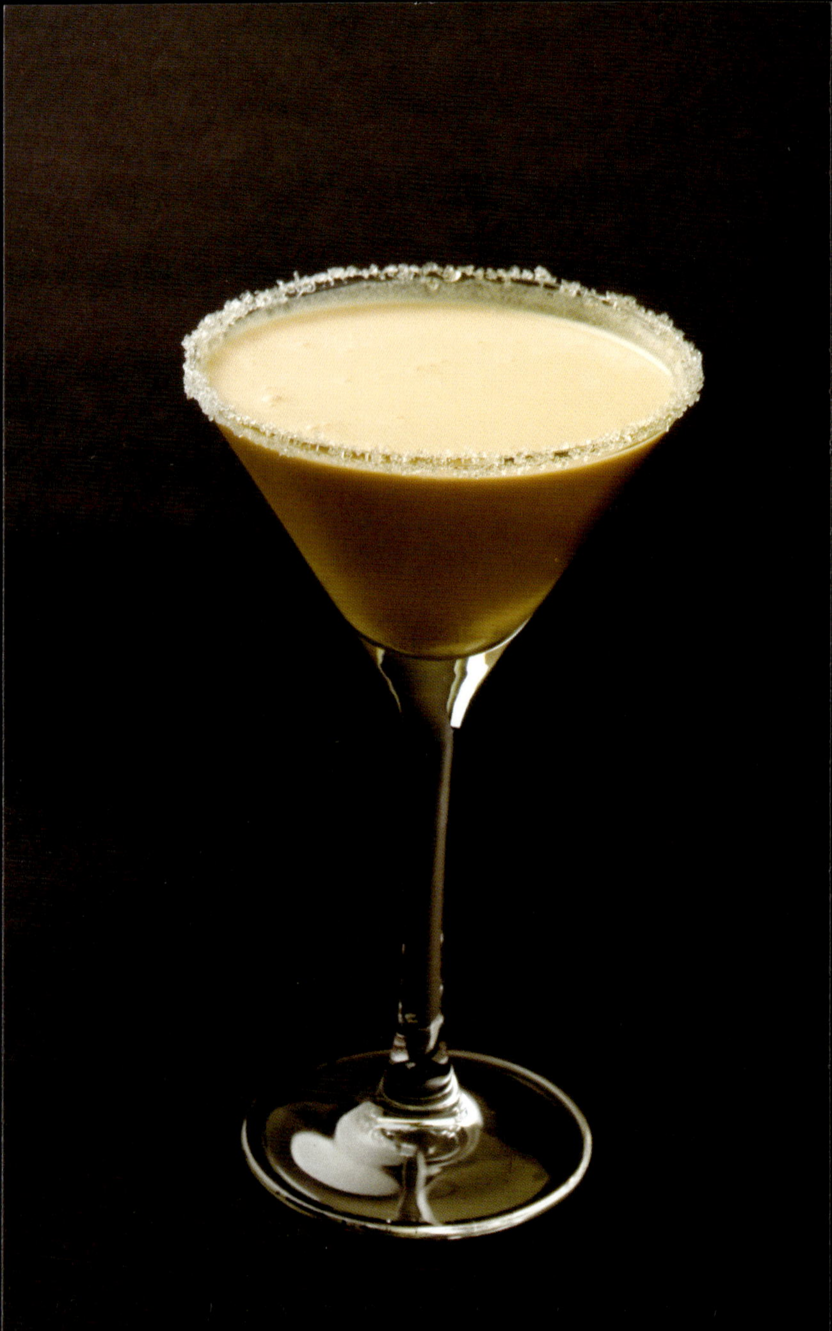

Vienna Soother

Ingredients:

Coffee	: 240 ml	Chocolate syrup	: 15 ml
Cream	: 120 ml	Ice as required	
Cinnamon	: ½ tsp		

Procedure:
1) Pour the ingredients into an ice filled cocktail shaker.
2) Shake it well.
3) Strain into a glass.
4) If desired top it with whipped cream and shaved chocolate.
5) Serve it chilled.

Baby Bellini

Ingredients:

Chilled peach nectar	: 60 ml	Fresh lemon juice	: 30 ml
Sparkling apple cider	: 60 ml		

Procedure:
1) Pour both Peach nectar and fresh Lemon juice into a glass.
2) Stir well.
3) Add Cider to the rim and stir again gently.
4) Serve it chilled.

Roogeltea

Ingredients:

Diet Root Beer	: 355 ml	Ice cubes	: 6 ice
Peach Ice		Light cream	: 125 ml
Tea (already mixed)	: 355 ml		

Procedure:
1) Add all ingredients to a blender and blend for approx 20 seconds.
2) Serve chilled.

The Tropical Spritzer

Ingredients:

Strawbery juice	: 50 ml	Orange juice	: 40 ml
Kiwi juice	: 45 ml	Soda water to top	
Lime juice	: 45 ml	Ice as required	

Procedure:

1) In a cocktail glass filled with ice, add the juices and mix.
2) Top with soda water and stir gently.
3) If desired garnish with lime.

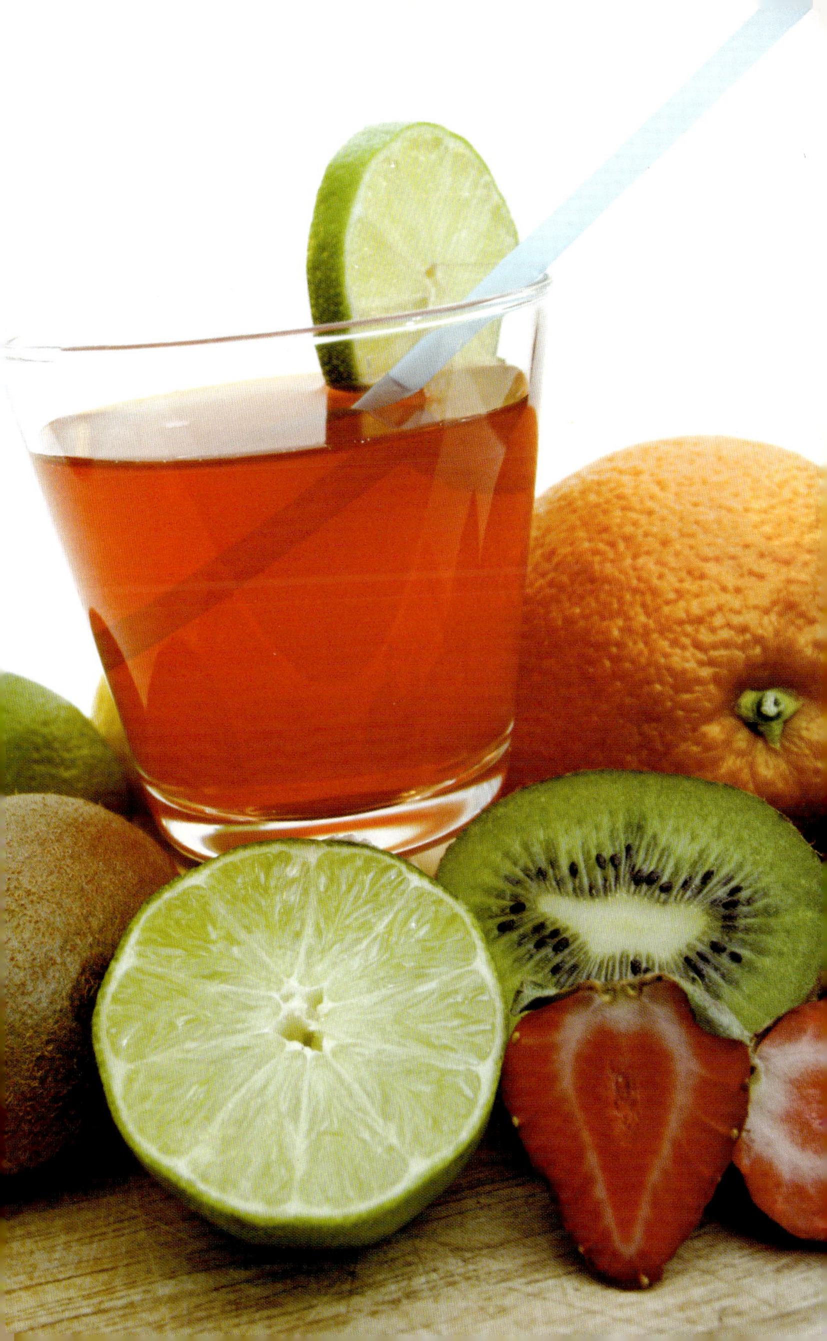

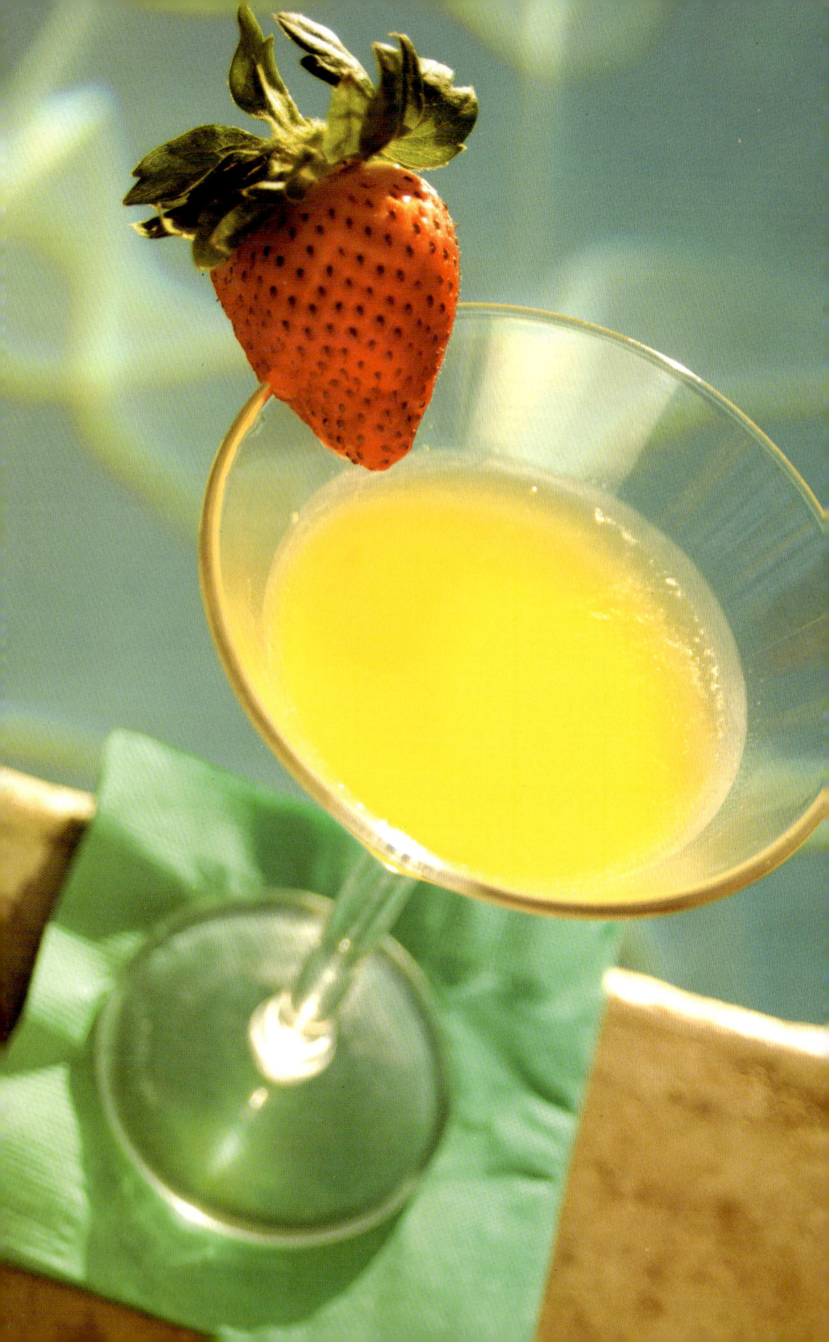

Virgin Mango Bellini

Ingredients:

Mangoes (diced & peeled) : 1 Cup	Ginger Ale (Ginger flavored
Fresh lime juice : 2½ tbsp	carbonated soft drink) : 2 Cups
Grenadine : 2 tsp	Chilled sugar syrup : 6 tbsp

Procedure:
1) Put mangoes in a blender.
2) Then add lemon juice and sugar syrup.
3) Mix it until smooth.
4) Strain the mango puree and discard pulp.
5) Pour the mango puree in a glass.
6) Add ginger ale and grenadine.
7) Stir and serve it chilled.

The English Garden Sipper

Ingredients:

Iced tea	: 120ml	Fresh raspberries as needed
Raspberry juice	: 120 ml	Ice as required
Fresh lemon	: 1 wedge	

Procedure:
1) Fill a cooler glass with ice.
2) Pour the iced tea and raspberry juice on top.
3) Garnish with fresh lemon and raspberries.

The Berry Patch

Ingredients:

Vanilla ice cream	: 2 scoops	Fresh strawberries	: a few
Fresh blueberries	: a few	Milk	: ½ cup
Fresh raspberries	: a few		

Procedure:

1) In a blender, add the vanilla ice cream with all the fresh fruits and ½ cup milk.
2) Blend thoroughly and strain into a tumbler or martini glass.
3) Sprinkle with fresh berries and serve.

Hot Fudge Sundae

Ingredients:

Italian caramel syrup	: 15 ml
Italian strawberry syrup	: 15ml
Hot chocolate drink	: 240 ml

Whipped cream as desired
Chocolate sauce as desired
Cherry to garnish

Procedure:
1) Pour into a large heatproof mug or glass the two syrups, and top with the hot chocolate.
2) Garnish with whipped cream, a drizzle of chocolate sauce and a cherry.

Note:
- *Hot chocolate drink can be made using the hot chocolate pre-mix available at gourmet stores.*

Virgin Strawberry Daiquiri

Ingredients:

Strawberries	: ¼ cup	Sugar	: 2 tsp
Orange juice	: 30 ml	Dash of grenadine	
Lime juice	: 30 ml	Ice as required	

Procedure:
1) Pour all ingredients in a blender with ice.
2) Blend on medium speed for a few seconds.

To serve: Pour into daiquiri glass and garnish with mint leaves.

Quiet Passion

Ingredients:

White grape juice	: 90 ml	Passion fruit juice	: 30 ml
Grapefruit juice	: 90 ml	Ice as required	

Procedure:
1) Fill a cocktail shaker half with ice.
2) Pour all the ingredients into it.
3) Shake for as long as it takes to froth slightly.
4) Serve chilled.

To serve: *Pour and serve in tall glass.*

Bikini Breezer

Ingredients:

Strawberries	: 1 cup	Banana, ripe	: 1
Skim milk	: 1 cup	Crushed ice as required	
Orange juice	: 1 cup		

Procedure:

1) Pour all ingredients into a blender jar, except the ice.
2) Whirl away till smooth.
3) Add the crushed ice and process for just a few seconds.

Fruity Punch

(Preparation for a party)

Ingredients:

Frozen cranberry juice	: 2 cups	Pineapple juice	: 2 cups
Water	: 6 cups	Ginger ale	: 4 litres
Orange juice	: 2 cups		

Procedure:

1) Combine all the juices and chill in the refrigerator.
2) Then pour into a punch bowl over a large block of ice.
3) Top with ginger ale.

Unfuzzy Navel

Ingredients:

Peach Nectar	: 90 ml	Lemon juice	: 1 tsp
Orange juice	: 90 ml	Grenadine	: a dash
Pineapple juice	: 90 ml	Ice as required	

Procedure:

1) Fill cocktail shaker half with ice.
2) Combine all ingredients in the shaker.
3) give a quick shake to blend nicely.
4) Serve chilled.

To serve: *Pour in a pre chilled glass.*

Tequila Meadow

Ingredients:

Orange juice	: 60 ml	Lemon/lime soda	: 60 ml
Pineapple juice	: 60 ml	Grenadine	: 8 ml
Cranberry juice	: 15 ml	Ice as required	

Procedure:
1) Fill a cocktail shaker half with ice.
2) Combine all ingredients in the shaker except the soda.
3) Strain out in a glass and top with soda.
4) Serve chilled.

Notes

Notes

ALSO AVAILABLE

STAR Rasoi Cook Books

Punjabi Swaad
Punjabi Vegetarian Cooking

Kukkad- E-josh
Chicken Recipes of Punjab

Acharon Ka Mela
Indian Pickles

Khomche Ke Chatoriya
Indian Streetfood

Dosai
Dosa Delights

Wazwan-e-kashmiriyat
Kashmiri Recipes

Gehun Ke Rang
Indian Rotis, Naans & Paranthas

Dhaba Stop
Dhaba Delights

Gujarat Nu
Gujarati Recipes

Smoking Delights
Grills & Sizzlers

Dabba Khana
Lunchbox Recipes

Aadab-e-biryani
Indian Biryanis

Pachakam
Kerala Cooking

Classic Flavours
Continental Cuisine

Piknik Khaana
Picnic Meals

Seven Culinary Tastes
North-eastern India Recipes

Chingri Tales
Prawn Recipes

Kaliyo, Ghonto And Dalna
Bengali Recipes

Mishti Mookh
Bengali Festival Sweets

Sagar Se
Goan Seafood Curries

Karwari Delicacies
Malabar & Konkan Cooking

Registaan Ke Pakvaan
Banjara Recipes From Rajasthan

Hare Pattoan Ka Saag
Saag Recipies

ALSO AVAILABLE

STAR Rasoi Cook Books

Daal-e-dilkhush
Indian Lentil Dishes

Aadab-e-lazeez
Mughlai Cooking

Call Of The Orient
Chinese Cooking

Flavors Of Thailand
Thai Cooking

Crusts And Swirls!
Pizzas & Pastas

Sweet Savories
Continental Desserts

Morning Fiesta
Breakfast Meals

Shaakahari Khana
Indian Vegetarian Cooking

Chilled Concoctions
Shakes And Smoothies

Stirring Tales!
Mocktails

Pouring Fantasies
Cocktails

Fires From The Clay Oven!
Tandoori Delights

Flavours of Italia
Italain Cooking

FUTURE TITLES

Oriental Soups & Starters
Continental Soups & Starters
Sandwiches & Wraps
Mexican Cooking
Asian Curries
Diet Cooking
Microwave Cooking
Baby Cook book
Tamil Cooking
Navratra ka Khana
Khichdies
Sinhalese Cooking
Puddings
Andhra Cooking
Orissa Cooking
Garhwal Ka Fanaa
Maharashtrian Khanna
Cooking with Wines & Sherry
Coconut based Cooking
Bong Mustard in your meals
Mediterranean Cooking

& many more